Lazy Susanne
(like a lazy Susan, but for Poetry)

Marcus Kahle McCann

BookLeaf Publishing

India | USA | UK

Presentation by *BookLeaf Publishing*

Web: www.bookleafpub.com

E-mail: info@bookleafpub.com

ISBN: 9789360944063

First edition 2024

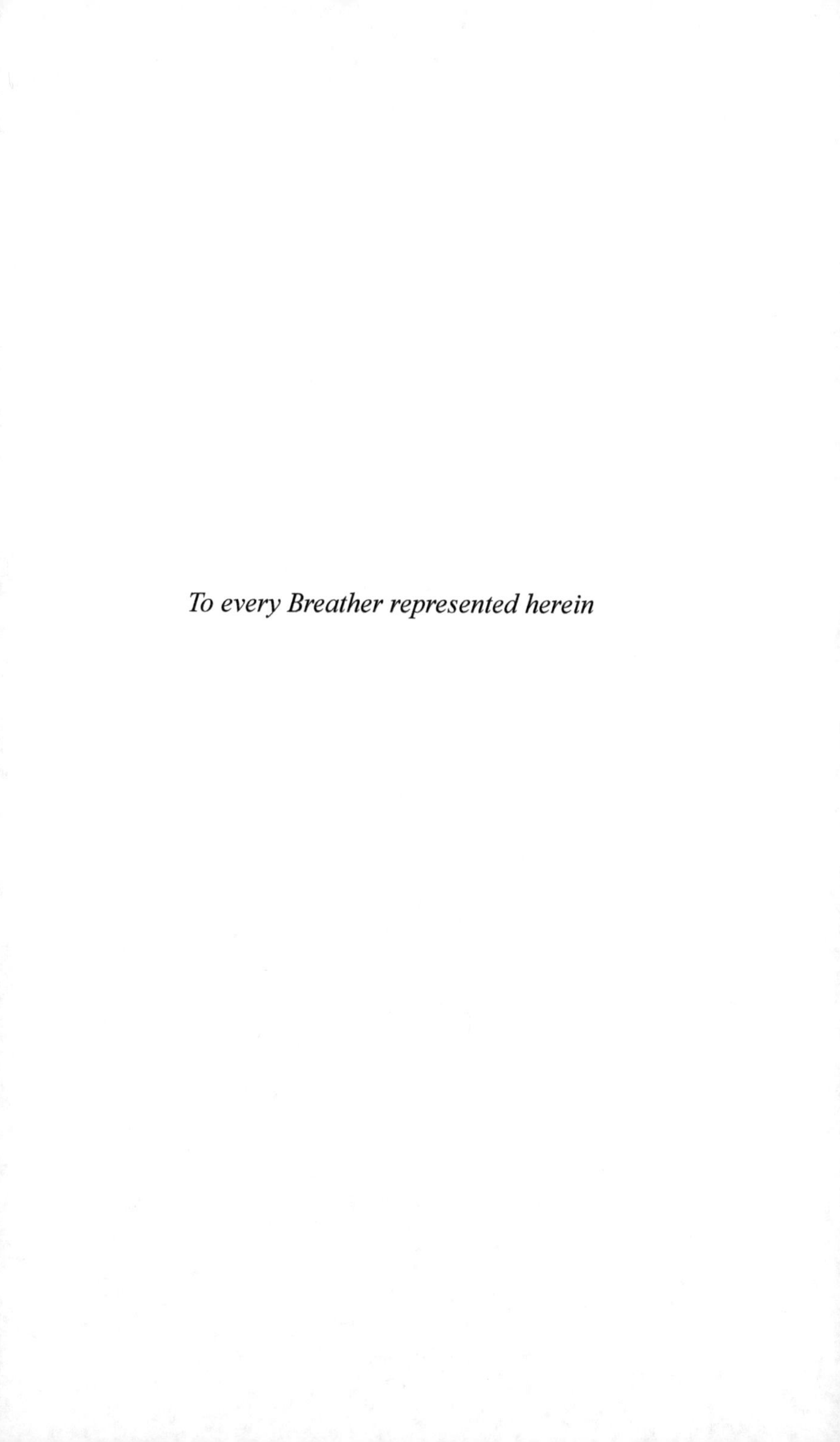

To every Breather represented herein

ACKNOWLEDGEMENT

Thank you to BookLeaf for the challenge; and a bigger, more heartfelt Thank you to my wife, Becky, who encouraged me to start the challenge and then enabled me to finish it!

PREFACE

Each poem here is inspired by a friend or family member or by being a friend and family member. Of course I'm referring to my friends and family specifically, but I wouldn't be surprised if you find your own friends and family in here too and maybe something of yourself.

Mommy is a Lullaby

1

Mommy is a Lullaby
In
And of
Herself

Snow

The
      Snow
           Falls

     Slow

  and

slight

     And

        in the Sun

      She shimmers
            Bright

       Atop the Wind

              And softest sigh
        Lofty

       Lilting

        By the Bye

       Lofty
        Lilting
      By
        The
      Bye

    She Flits   And Flutters

                    Sleek
                And
        Sly

                Deftly
                    Dancing
            In the Light

                        This

                Downward

                        Drifting

                Wedding

                White
            Her Blanket
    Waiting There to Lie Cool and Cozy By The Bye

Wedding Vows

Today I Vow
To honor and to keep you
To cherish
and to treat you Well
I pledge you my heart
'Til death do us part.

Until you are dead
We'll be together

Until you are dead
We'll be as one

But after you're dead
I guess that's it then
Just call it quits and
be done

Today I Vow
To have you and hold you
To hear you and to know you and tell
You
that I'm yours and you're mine
'til one of us dies

Until you are dead
I'll be faithful

Until you are dead
I'll be true

But after you're dead
I should probably move on
And find somebody new

If you're sick or healthy
If we're poor or wealthy
I'll lay down my life for you
I would even die for you
If that's what it took
And after that
you're off the hook

Until you are dead
I'll be committed

Until you are dead
I'll see things through

But after you're dead
I'll still love you

Today I Vow
To encourage and embrace you

All my life to face you
Myself
For better or worse

....Unless you go first

50 Years

It's been 50 years
Of Better and worse
Having and holding,
Half things and whole things
And finding hidden Blessings in curses

It's been 50 years
Of sickness and health
Hard work and hardships,
Tempered contentment
And some loose interpretations of wealth

It's been 50 years
Of despair and delight
Laughter and tears
Too many careers
And Walking more by faith than by sight

But mostly Love
Love like a fountain
like a fire
like a fortress on a hill
Love that's sacrificial
stands in the middle
love that always perseveres
This is how you've loved

and It's been 50 years
Yes, Some of them longer than others
After some time
This husband and wife
Became a father and mother.

It's been 50 years
of shaping the lives
of young ones and old ones
broken ones and whole ones
and teaching both the foolish and wise

It's been 50 years
of singing a song
telling a story
of grace and of glory
And building a home where all can belong

Now look at this thing you've made
Look at this thing you've made
Look at this thing you've made
with your love
Look at this thing you've made
all of us

Dancers and dreamers
and builders and writers
musicians and athletes

and singers and fighters
healers and helpers
good mothers and fathers
teachers and students
good sons and good daughters

that Love like a fountain
like a fire
like a fortress on a hill
Love that's sacrificial
stands in the middle
love that always perseveres
'cause this is how you've loved
and this is how you love
so this is how you're loved

Gale

I looked into the eyes of the Storm
And saw that she loved me

The Laborer

She works with her hands
Deft and Diligent
Gentle and Inevitable
She works with her eyes
Seeing Opportunities
And Potential
She works with her lips
Teaching
And speaking Encouragements
She works with her Heart
Compassionate and understanding
Patient and Warm
She labors
She works with her hands and her heart
Her eyes and her lips
With the tools of her self
In the forge of her being
She shapes new Life

The Goose, The Gander, The Salamander

The Goose, The Gander, The Salamander

Through the stars doth he meander
the Goose, the Gander,
the Salamander.

When Night assails
he withstands her
The Goose, The Gander,
The Salamander

Kind and Courageous
a smile his answer
The Goose, The Gander,
The Salamander

He Speaks the Truth
with Grace and Candor
The Goose, The Gander,
The Salamander

A gentleman true
Ne'er to philander
The Goose, The Gander,
The Salamander

Light and Life
fly as his banner
this Goose,
this Gander,
this little Salamander

Morning Drake

What luck!
A Duck,
A Drake on a lake
Paddling peacefully by

What fun!
A Son,
Another one,
A Prince of the water and sky

Ahoy!
A Boy
A yonder joy
Aloft on adventurous wings

Too right!
A light
A well-whetted wit
And a laugh birds wish they could sing

Compassionate, clever,
Sincere and so strong
Smiles for miles
This duck of the dawn

This
Light of
Mine

The mountains will melt like wax beneath my feet
as I dance
like fire on a candle.
And the sun will be covered
When my voice rises
Like smoke
My heart will lay like a wick in scented oil
And I will be consumed

Driveway

See how she
Stands solitarily
Waiting for a man to come home
Hugging her knees
Between her house and the street
Wishing she wasn't alone

But she is
She's a rebel
And nothing but trouble
And she'll never be anything else
Born in the middle
And ever since she was little
She's wanted to be by herself

Notice the way
She stands solipsistically
Waiting for Christ to return
She falls to her knees
Between her house and the street
Because her lessons
Are hard ones to learn

What if
She's a rebel

And nothing but trouble
And she'll never be anything else
So she wades to the altar
On her brother's weak shoulders
Drowning the lies that she's held

See how she
Throws her hands up
Triumphantly
As if reaching for someone to hold
There's blood on her knees
But her body is free
Because no one can steal what she knows

That
She's not a rebel
A witch or a devil
And she's not alone in the least

She's simply a girl
Growing up in this driveway
That connects
her house
to the street

A Man Who Builds

I've waged the good warfare
With this hammer I have
This hammer I carry
In these masculine hands

I've made and destroyed
Built up and torn down
I've stirred dust in the air
And spilled blood on the ground

This hammer has trained me
Since the days of my youth
To strike fast and strike strong
And strike only in truth

I've routed an army
And conquered the land
Won the heart of a woman
And done the work of a man

And if I should walk
This entire world wide
And all of creation
Fall under my stride
I'd grip tight my hammer

This hammer of mine
And we'd war the good warfare
My hammer and I.

Felion

I knew a Felion that lived in the jungle
She loved running and jumping
And sometimes to snuggle.
I remember this creature of such power and
grace
With a big lion's body and a little girl's face
And how the first time I saw her
I was a little disturbed
Though I was soon to discover
My fear was absurd
Because she was kind and polite and not savage
at all
And in social settings she was the bell of the ball
In beauty and balance not one could surpass her
It was hardly a wonder she was such a fine
dancer.
She was majestic in battle, full of courage and
might
Just as brave in the darkness as she was in the
light
Oh how I long
for those days that I saw her
I think of her often and each time grow fonder.
In case my words are obscure
Or their meanings too subtle

She is the reason
I miss my time in the jungle.

Dug He Deeper Down

One time I met a man
made of many rubber bands
he had straps of arms for leather
and articulated hands
He had a swagger like a swindle
like a lying liar should
And the timbre of a timber
like a slowly falling wood
He had a cackle in his laughing
like the cracking of a branch
and his face was like the foretaste
of a complicated past
whether withered by the weather
warmer bones were never borne,
bared, or broken in a body
stretching bending like a home.

Here, Today

I'm sad, Today,
because I've been unkind to you
and never given you the time you were due,
the time I owed.
I've taken you for granted
never truly appreciated you.
I've traded the reality of you for the fantasy of
Tomorrow;
and this,
I fear,
is unforgivable.
I've feared that for a long time;
yet,
to my shame and amazement,
you're always here for me.
Always.

Such a Jewel Am I

I've been cut
So you can see me
So you can see my many faces
I've been set
In polished silver
Laid in black and satin places
I've been sold
To certain persons
Of pure pedigree and charm
And I've been worn
By wealthy women
With weak and weary arms

I can shine
Or simply shimmer
Catch the eye with subtle glimmers
I can bounce
The light or bend it
Either fight it or defend it
And I can prove
My worth with scarcity
With poise and form and clarity

Precious
And luxurious

I
Am
Beautiful

Look at the Boy that Looks
Like a Fox

Look at me RUN
Because I'm *fast as a fox*
So   *swift*   like   a   fox.
I'm quickas afox.

                       M
                 U   P
Look at me J
Because I'm spRY like a fox
                           Just

as fleet as a fox
I'm L I T H E like a fox

Look at me reason
Because I'm _{keen} as a fox
Very Wise like a fox

I'm sly as a fox

Now look at me
And see that you see
That I am not a fox
But a BOY
Indeed, a young man
Of a certain sTature and poise
With all the same features as other such boys.

Now let me be clear

These are not paws that I have
                    But two beautiful feet and
          two capable hands

               That just so happen
to be cleverly hidden
               By these fuzzy black socks
          And these black woolen mittens

          And I assure you this coat
          (That is red like bright passion)
          I wear <u>only</u> for warmth!
....And
          sometimes for fashion.

                    E   i
               y   a   o   n
          M   rs are not p   ted

My T   h are not   rp
      e   t   S   a
         e   h

          My tail is not *bushy*
          And it's rare that I BARK

                    no

I AM NOT A FOX
I don't plot or connive

I   am   only a MaN   With   m i
s c h i e v o u s   e y e s

But Never-you-mind
        these mischievous eyes
For if you look **deep** behind them
You'll find nothing but kindness

Because I'm

s o f t

as a fox

Truly   **warm**

like a fox

I'm LIGHT
as a fox

Look at me

Because I look like a fox
            Just enough like a fox

I'm a boy like a fox.

Two Hearts are Better...

29

My heart was won
By my firstborn son
So for his brother,
I grew another.

Tired

The train of thought so often derails
I forget how to think and all it entails
The madness is the method
I firmly believe
That a tattered old shirt with a random heart on
the sleeve
Can give us the answer
To what I don't know
But the train is now leaving
With no place to go

Bones

When you're no longer pretty
And my heart beat has slown
When your eyes have stopped shining
And the distance has grown
When you're wrinkled and withered
And our morning's unknown
I will reach for your skin
And find nothing but bones

I will reach for your skin and find nothing but
bones
Slender, they are, and brittle and cold
My fingers will settle on dry, dusty bones

When we've stopped all our whispers
And the love birds have flown
When we've put out the fires
That burned in our home
When the lies are uncovered
And all secret things shown
I will gaze in amazement
On your milky, white bones

I will gaze in amazement on your milky, white
bones

Fragile, they are, and broken and old
My attention will settle on small, sharpened
bones

When you've lost all your marbles
And I've dropped all my stones
When we've forgotten the passion
The gasps and the groans
When you've wasted away
And I'm feeling alone
To what should I cling
But your comfortable bones?

To what should I cling but your comfortable
bones?
Awkward, they are, and thoroughly known
My affection will settle on beautiful bones

Jibberjum

Oh what, chummy chum, is a Jibberjum?
What but the sum of a jibber and a jum

like the sound of a tummy
Being drummed like a drum
or Heartstrings strummed
Thrrum thrrum
Thrrum thrrum

Or the trundle of a mumble
Of a bungled banter flung

Or a zinger like the stinger
On a humble bumble's bum

Maybe a bundle full of bindles
Fumble tumbling from the thumb

Or a yummy honey crumble
On a Monday on the tongue

It could mean more
It might mean none
Such
is the puzzle of the Jibberjum

words

I've got words,
So help me,
words and words.
Words
that stir the dirt
or
silence violent thoughts.
I've got words
that spread like honey
or
that make a big one small.
I've got words,
such words,
you've never heard
said in such a way.
and
They are cheap
but
never easy.
And…
that's all I have to say.